The University of Liverpool

Its Present State

I. INTRODUCTORY.

IT is not quite four years since the Royal charter was granted which turned Liverpool into the seat of an independent University. It is a little more than twenty-five years since the University College, out of which the University has sprung, opened its doors. This seems, therefore, an appropriate moment at which to review the present state of the institution, and to ask what has been the outcome of twenty-five years of work and of generous support?

It was a heroic enterprise—many thought, and some, perhaps, still think, it was a hopelessly quixotic enterprise—to attempt to plant a great University in a city like Liverpool. The initiators of the enterprise had to anticipate a flood of ridicule and depreciation from captious critics without faith or imagination. They faced all that, and achieved their dream in spite of it. It is not easy to imagine a contrast more impressive than that between the nobly generous men who set out, in face of vast obstacles, to create for their city a University that should be worthy of its greatness, and, on the other hand, those armchair critics who aired their cleverness by cheap sneers and misrepresentations.

It may be worth while, at the outset, to summarise the difficulties which faced (and to some extent still face) the enterprise. In the first place, the English people have not yet learnt that sense of the value and power of knowledge which is the secret of the success of Scotland, Germany, and America. It is only recently that they have been converted to a belief in the value of elementary education for the people at large; the value of high scientific training for those who have to work with their brains—the value of this not only for the workers themselves, but still more for the community in which they work, the English people had yet to learn when University College was founded. And nowhere was this dangerous scepticism more widespread than in Lancashire. University education had so long been the privilege of the few that it was generally regarded as a luxury proper only for the well-to-do; a graceful ornament, not a necessity for national efficiency. The idea of a type of University like those on which Germany and America are building their greatness, which should seriously set itself to grapple with the problems of modern life, and to provide scientific training for all the new scientific professions which the conditions of modern life have called into being—such an idea had not begun to be widely understood. For the Englishman's notion of a University was solely founded upon Oxford and Cambridge, and because Oxford and Cambridge principally taught the classics and mathematics, it was supposed that these were almost the only subjects which a University could or ought to teach.

Moreover the social prestige of the ancient Universities was so overwhelmingly strong that all the snobbish elements in English society—and how numerous these are!—were likely to laugh at the very idea of sending their sons anywhere else. The founders of the new institution might anticipate that most upper-middle-class parents would prefer to see their sons do without a University education altogether if they could not have the social advantages of Oxford and Cambridge; that they would not for worlds allow their sons to run the risk of contamination by sitting beside the sons of tradesmen or of working men. As for these latter, the habit of expecting their children to begin earning money at an early age was so deeply rooted in this district that few of them could be expected to undergo the very real sacrifice of keeping their sons at unproductive pursuits for three or four years. Thus, for one reason or another, the founders of the new University could not expect to see students in very large numbers flocking to their classes, for the public had first to be educated. Yet from the very first the numbers were far higher than anybody had a right to expect, which conclusively showed how great was the need.

A further difficulty arose from the fact that secondary education in this district was in an extremely backward condition, so that the majority even of those students who did come were apt to be inadequately prepared. They might be (and often were) men of mature minds and considerable ability. But they had not had a fair chance of obtaining a good school training, and it appeared to be impossible to exact from them at first the standard at entrance which a University ought to impose. The consequence was that the University College had for a number of years to undertake part of the work of a school as well as the work of a University. That has now wholly ceased, but while it lasted it naturally aroused the hostility of those schools which were conducted on a high standard, and with which the College (against its will) appeared to be competing. Many thought that this condition of things showed that the College had been prematurely founded, and that the system of secondary education should first have been perfected. The answer to this was (and is) that one of the causes for the backwardness of secondary education is the absence of a sufficient supply of highly-trained teachers, a defect which can only be met by the institution of Universities.

Finally, any new University must be heavily handicapped by the fact that it has to stand comparison not only with the social prestige, but with the immense resources, of the old Universities—resources which have been accumulated during many centuries. The University and colleges of Oxford enjoy among them an income (roughly estimated) of about £400,000, yet Oxford is complaining, with much justice, of its inadequate endowment. Lord Curzon is appealing for a quarter of a million sterling to meet immediate needs, and the Government has been urged to give to that venerable University a subsidy of £100,000 per annum—a sum, it may be noted, equal to the total

B

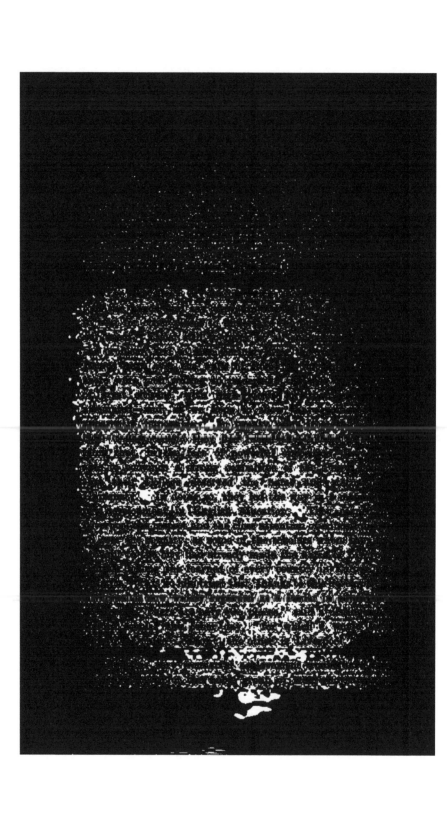

and maintained the University in its early days. It was the fact that the power and wealth of the second city in the kingdom was arrayed in its favour which determined the issue. What decided the Privy Council to grant a charter to the University was not merely the evidence (under searching cross-examination) of the good work which it was doing, but, still more, the unanimous demand of the City Council, which in the action which it then took gave a lead to the cities of England; for, though Liverpool led the way, she stands now by no means alone. The City Council declared that Liverpool needed a University. The City Council pledged itself to ensure that the University should be a worthy one by giving it from the public purse that financial support which was necessary to make up for the lack of ancient endowments. In fulfilment of that pledge the Council has given an annual subsidy of £10,000 to the University, and has been more intimately associated with its control and government than the ruling authority of any city had ever before been associated in the government of a University. And as the City Council is responsible for the existence of the University, it rightly and naturally possesses the fullest powers of criticism and inspection. Not only do five members appointed by the Council sit as members of the University Council and share in the discussion of every step that is taken, but an expert report, drawn up, after full inspection, at the Council's request, has been provided by Sir Thomas Raleigh and the Master of Downing College, Cambridge.

That report is a most cordial and satisfactory appreciation of the work of the University. But as it does not attempt to describe that work in detail, it will be the object of these papers to draw a picture of the University at the moment of its semi-jubilee, the end of the first stage in its development: its students, their numbers, where they come from, what they study, and what they do when they leave; its teachers and their work; its systems of instruction and the extent to which it fulfils the duty of adding to knowledge; its buildings and equipment; its finance; its mode of government; and the general services which it renders to the city. In short, we shall try to answer the questions: Was the University worth establishing? Is it worth supporting? What work is it doing, and how is it doing it?

II. THE STUDENTS.

The most obvious test of the progress and efficiency of a University is to be found in the number of students who utilise it.   It is not an infallible test, because there are many other things to be considered, and some of the most highly-esteemed Universities have but a small number of students.   Thus no American University has a higher reputation in the learned world than Johns Hopkins University, Baltimore, yet it has only 720 students all told; while the ancient Scottish University of St. Andrews has only 320.   Still, numbers are a good rough test of progress.   Here are figures showing the number of students in the University of Liverpool at intervals of five years since its foundation :—

1882	...	117	1897	....	497
1887	...	315	1902	...	713
1892	...	411	1907	...	1004

These figures show a growth which is both rapid and steady.   In twenty-five years our University has attained the four figures, and is all but equal to Trinity College, Dublin (1,017), and only a little below Aberdeen (given as "about" 1,100).   That is a remarkable achievement.   But the figures scarcely show its full extent.   It will be noticed that the largest increase has been in the last five years, mainly since the College became a University.   Now in this period a great change was effected which tended to retard the increase of students.   Up till 1903 students were allowed to count a year's work for the matriculation examination towards the three years required for the degree, and the classes provided for this purpose, in which the work was practically school work, were among the largest in the College.   This system had been permitted, and, indeed, required, by the regulations of the Victoria University, of which Liverpool was a part.   But when that University was dissolved a clause was inserted in the charters of all the new Universities forbidding them to allow prematriculation

of a University. A few of them hold post-graduate fellowships, but these are of small pecuniary amount—not nearly as much as the abilities of the holders would enable them to earn; so that it must be a real zeal for knowledge which inspires them. In no case is the Fellowship of greater value than £100 per annum, excepting the " 1851 Scholarship," provided by the trustees of the surplus from the Great Exhibition.

Next come a large group of students aiming at diplomas or certificates granted either by the University itself or by other bodies to students taking courses which lead up to particular professions. Such students exist in large numbers in almost every University, for it is an entire fallacy to suppose that all students in a University are aiming at the degrees of the University. The principal groups of these students may be briefly enumerated. There are architects, who take a full two years' course; engineers, who take a course extending over either two or three years; medical students preparing for the diplomas of the Royal Colleges of Physicians and Surgeons; students of dentistry preparing for the qualification of L.D.S.; students of veterinary medicine—the last three groups taking a course extending over at least five years; and students of law preparing for their qualifications as solicitors or for the bar examinations. All these are perfectly serious students, being prepared for exacting professions, in which the effectiveness of their training may be of the most material importance to the industries of the country, or the comfort, health, or interests of thousands of people. It surely needs no demonstration that the University does a great public service in providing them with the highest possible training. Some people ignorantly imagine that it is no part of the business of a University to train such students. But that is a mere fallacy. In the first place, nearly every University does this kind of work. In the second place, if the University did not do it, it would not be done at all. Either the students would go untrained, or they would have to go elsewhere, or the city would have to provide facilities otherwise. The city could not provide any adequate facilities except at an expenditure of very much more than £10,000 per annum.

Lastly, the thousand students include a small number of persons taking only two or three courses. Some of these are young men or young women who have had their full school course, but who, while they do not wish to spend the three years required for taking a degree, are anxious to obtain some further culture. Others are cultivated professional and business men, or leisured ladies, who take the advantage of the opportunities which the University affords for widening their intellectual interests. A good many of them, for example, are enthusiasts in archæology, in which the University of Liverpool now possesses an equipment for teaching unequalled in Britain. This equipment has been provided entirely by the generosity of a few great merchants and ladies, and is not at all derived from the city grant.

The great mass of these thousand students come, naturally, from Liverpool and its immediate vicinity. But it would be a very unhealthy sign if there were none but local students. It is a tribute to the efficiency of the University that there is a fair proportion of students from a distance. Most of the counties of England are represented by one or two students. A few come from Scotland, passing the doors of Edinburgh and Glasgow, and one or two from Ireland. There is also a sprinkling of foreign students: France, Spain, Germany, Austria, Sweden, China, Egypt, Canada, South America, West Africa, Cape Colony, and Australia have all had representatives within the last year or two. One little town in the north of Spain has had some students here in each of the last ten years, and at one time there were as many as seven students in various faculties from this one place. These students cost the city nothing; they come to take advantage of the facilities that have had to be provided for Liverpool students. But their presence is valuable, first, because it is good for the other students;

and, secondly, because it shows that the University has a high reputation not only outside of Liverpool, but outside of England.

A large majority of the students are comparatively poor men and women, who would not have been able to bear the cost of a University education but for the foundation of the University of Liverpool. They come principally from the middle-class schools, and a large proportion of them have been previously at the elementary schools. There is a large group from the Pupil Teachers' Colleges, especially the City College at Clarence Street; for the University—like every other University in Britain, including Oxford and Cambridge —prepares many students for elementary teaching. Every one of these students takes a full degree course. In Scotland a majority of the teachers training for elementary work take University courses; in England such courses are as yet taken by only a small minority.

Students whose parents have small means often experience considerable difficulty in bearing the burden of University courses. The University of Liverpool has only a small number of endowed scholarships to aid them; it is very ill-supplied in comparison with the Scottish Universities. The most valuable scholarships are those awarded by the City Council. Every holder of these scholarships, besides receiving a grant from the city, is admitted to courses in the University without fee. But, after all, scholarships are competitive, and the winners are not always those who stand most in need of aid. Hence an immense boon has been conferred upon poor students by the provision under which at least £1,000 per annum from the city grant is to be set aside for grants in aid to deserving students whose parents are ratepayers. These grants are administered with the utmost care, and no student is eligible for them who has not proved his competence. But without their aid many a good student would have lost the chance of a University education, or only attained it with severe hardships.

c

It must not, however, be supposed that all students here are poor. There is a substantial proportion of sons of well-to-do parents. The public school man is not very common, and he chiefly takes professional courses in medicine, engineering, architecture, or the like. But students of this type, who require no aid, are steadily increasing in numbers. Nevertheless, on the whole, the University of Liverpool is a democratic University. It is a University of the people— a University which opens careers to poor men—in a sense almost unknown in England until this generation.

Something ought to be said about the student-life of the University. Inevitably a non-residential University, whose students scatter in the evening to all parts of a wide area, stands at a disadvantage in this respect in comparison with the residential Universities. This is particularly felt in games, for it is hard to persuade the student to return in his free time. Nevertheless, the students have themselves developed a remarkable social life of their own, quite different in character from that of the old Universities. It is not imitative; it is spontaneous, original, and characteristic. There is probably no non-residential University in England where student-life is so vigorous, or so happily organised; and the delegates from other Universities who recently attended the British students' congress held in Liverpool all expressed their deep admiration for the system of self-government and social life which our students have developed. Every student is a member of the Guild of Undergraduates, and pays annually a subscription of 15s. The administration of this revenue, and the general direction of student affairs, is in the hands of a representative council, whose presidents are the recognised official spokesmen of the student body, and are supported with remarkable loyalty by that body. The magnitude and variety of the enterprises which they conduct are remarkable. They have clubs for every kind of athletics, all of which are freely open to all students. They run a fortnightly paper, which is distributed free to all students. They organise great debates, to which frequently representatives from other Universities are invited. On a recent

occasion every English and Welsh University except Oxford
sent representatives; and the attendance on these occasions
is very large. They have prepared a special song-book of
their own—a most interesting collection—which they use
'with great vigour at the delightful suppers and smoking
concerts and other festivities which they organise. All these
privileges are freely shared by all students in return for the
subscription of 15s.; and it will be admitted that this
represents a remarkable financial and administrative capacity.
Indeed, the training for business or public life which the
students give themselves by this direction of their own affairs
has no parallel, in the writer's knowledge, at any other
University. In addition to all this, they keep open, with
some outside aid, two small clubhouses—one for men and
one for women—managed by themselves. And the keenness
of their intellectual interests is shown by the fact that no
less than twenty small societies are kept going for the
discussion of the subjects with which their work is chiefly
concerned. Practically every group of subjects has its little
discussion club, in which the teachers sometimes take part,
but which is more often run entirely by the students
themselves. Practically every student is a member of one
or other of these clubs.

The student body is proudly conscious of the fact that
it is making the traditions of a new University, and is
resolved that these traditions shall be natural, healthy, and
inspiring. One of the principal notes is the cheerful
acceptance of a disciplined obedience to their own elected
leaders. Of this the public sees little, and if space permitted
it would deserve examination. Those who have visited
the pantomime on a students' night and heard how promptly
silence follows the president's whistle, if they have seen the
pandemonium which is created by other bodies of students
on such occasions, will realise what a striking thing this
voluntary discipline is. Naturally when some hundreds of
young men get together there is noise. Sometimes, but very
rarely, they get out of hand. Sometimes a few misbehave
themselves. But Liverpool students seem to have resolved

that among them there shall never be such orgies of disorder
as often reduce Scotch lecture-rooms to bear-gardens, or make
the streets near a Scotch University at the time of a Rectorial
election a terror to the timid, or burst forth in wild riot
after an Oxford bump-supper, or at a Socialist meeting in
Cambridge.

This article has so extended itself that little space is
left in which to describe what these students do when they
leave the University. That, however, will be brought out
in detail in a register of graduates which is soon to be
published. Here two sentences must suffice. It may be
taken as a sign of the quality of the students and their work
that within the last two years seven graduates of Liverpool
have been appointed professors in various Universities—in
classics, history, Sanskrit, chemistry, electrical engineering,
natural history, and comparative pathology—besides a score
of lecturers and other University teachers. Other graduates
are among the consulting physicians and surgeons of great
hospitals, they are medical officers of health, they are directing
great engineering works in all parts of the world, they are
head masters of grammar schools and elementary schools,
they are inspectors and educational administrators, they are
Government officials, they are clergymen and lawyers, they
are successful business men—in short, all over the world,
but above all in Liverpool itself, they are serving the
community in all kinds of useful employments.

III. THE TEACHING BODY.

" I will found a University," said Cornell, the creator
of one of the noblest of modern American Universities,
" where all persons can obtain instruction in all subjects."
That is the ideal of a modern University. But it is an
ideal very difficult to attain, because it implies the existence
of at least as many teachers as there are subjects. It is
an axiom of University organisation that no one should be
permitted to teach who is not an authority on his subject,
or at least capable of forming an independent judgment by
independent criticism of the evidence. The number of
teachers is scarcely at all governed by the number of students;
it is governed by the number of subjects in which teaching
is offered. And so it is a fair test of the efficiency of a
University to ask : How many subjects does it teach? How
many specialists does it provide for the instruction of its
students?

If we count up all who are in one way or another enrolled
upon the teaching staff of the University, we shall find that
the total reaches the very respectable figure of 186. This
may at first sight seem very large, but it is small in comparison
with the number of teachers in many other places. And
when we analyse this large body, we find that the great
majority do not make their livelihood out of their University
teaching, but give their services honorarily or for a merely
nominal remuneration. The number of teachers—professors,
lecturers, and assistants—who devote the whole of their
time to teaching work, and get their livelihood from it, is
only seventy-seven, and they naturally undertake the main
burden of the teaching of the University. In addition,
there are ten professors and others who hold endowed posts
which have been founded by various benefactors primarily
for the purpose of encouraging research : the three chairs
of archæology and the chair of bio-chemistry may be given
as examples. The holders of these posts conduct research
themselves—the archæologists, for example, spend part of

every year digging in Egypt, Greece, or elsewhere—but they also afford guidance and direction to others who are willing to undertake such investigation. Most of them also offer a certain amount of instruction for undergraduates; but this is not the primary purpose for which these posts were instituted.

The remaining ninety-nine teachers (more than half of the total) are all men who are engaged in other professions or pursuits besides University teaching. Their presence in the teaching body is due to the deliberate policy which the University has followed of trying to make available for the use of students all the special knowledge and skill which the city possesses. The University would indeed have been much to blame if it had failed to take advantage of the readiness of many able and learned men in the city to aid in its work.

This large group of teachers may be divided into three sections. In the first place, there are twenty-five teachers of kindred or affiliated institutions whose teaching is recognised as being of University rank, so that students may count attendance on their courses under defined conditions towards the requirements for a degree or diploma. It would take too much space to explain in detail what these conditions are, and what affiliation means.

In the second place, twelve gentlemen of distinguished scholarship have received the title of "Honorary Reader" or "Honorary Lecturer," and very generously offer to give instruction in the special subjects upon which they are authorities—subjects which, as a rule, would otherwise be unrepresented. Thus, the late Dr. Lloyd was Reader in Phonetics; Mr. Sephton, so long the distinguished head of the Institute, offers instruction in a subject which he has made his own as Reader in Icelandic—naturally having only occasional students; Dr. Forbes, of the Public Museums, gives highly-valued occasional lectures as Reader in Ethnography; Mr. Plummer, of the Bidston Observatory, is Reader in Astronomy; and so on. Needless to say, while

these gentlemen cannot take part in the conduct of the
regular curriculum, the teaching which they give is of the
greatest value, and much enriches the University.

There yet remains the largest group—sixty-two teachers
who may be described as "professional," and whose teaching
is of the utmost importance and value in all those courses
which prepare students for particular professions. They are
most numerous in the Faculty of Medicine and its allied
schools, with which no less than fifty-three of the sixty-two
are connected. It is obvious that for professional training
such aid is not only invaluable, but indispensable. The
professor who does not practice can teach the student anatomy,
physiology, or pathology, and does so. But the practical
arts of medicine and surgery can only be taught effectively
by those who carry them on. When the student has finished
his theoretical teaching—when he has learnt to understand
the human body and its troubles as an object of calm and
scientific study—then he must follow the great physician or
the great surgeon round the hospitals, observe his treatment,
and listen to his explanations. It is the great good fortune
of the University of Liverpool that so large a number of
the leading medical specialists of the city share thus in the
work of training the future medical men. They do not all,
of course, teach all the students, but every student is
permitted to profit by their knowledge and experience if he
pleases. What applies in medicine applies, also, though in
a less degree, in other professions, such as engineering
and law.

When, however, we speak of the teaching body of the
University, we think primarily of the eighty-seven men and
women whose lifework is University teaching or research,
and who would not be in Liverpool at all if there were
no University. Of the eighty-seven, thirty-one are full
professors, holding endowed chairs, seven are "lecturers in
charge" of important subjects in which there is no endowed
chair, and the remainder are assistant lecturers of various
grades. A word ought to be said about the way in which

they are paid. And first let us take the professors, as distinguished from lecturers and assistants.

Four years ago, when the University became independent, all professors received a fixed salary, together with two-thirds of the fees paid by students attending their classes. The salaries thus paid ranged from £400 per annum to £1,500 per annum. This system, which had existed since the foundation of University College, was the usual system of all similar colleges. But it had several defects. The lower salaries were often insufficient to retain the permanent services of men of the highest standing, and consequently Liverpool had lost several brilliant teachers who ought to have been retained. On the other hand, the system of payment by fees, while it seemed to be the reward of attractive teaching, was really quite unjust. Though his work in other ways may be less, the professor of an unpopular subject has to give as much labour to the preparation of his lectures for small classes as the professor of a popular subject; moreover, there was a prospect that as the number of students grew, the salaries of the professors of those subjects which large numbers of students are bound to take would be swollen to a large amount, quite irrespective of the number of lectures they had to give or the ability of their teaching, and irrespective, also, of the additional assistance which the University would have to provide. The University, therefore, seized the opportunity of revising salary scales. The proportion of fees to be received by the professor was halved; in this modified form it was thought likely to be useful as an incentive. The sum of £600 per annum was fixed as the minimum salary (including fees) to be received by any professor. This is a very modest figure in comparison with the salaries paid, say, in the Scotch Universities, or with the earnings of successful professional men. On the other hand, £1,000 (including fees) was fixed as the maximum, in order to prevent the heaping up of unduly large salaries in the more popular subjects. This rearrangement involved at first some additional expenditure. But in the course of a few years it will rectify itself, and probably in the end turn out to be an economy. In any case, it gives the University a much freer hand in dealing with fees.

The University next went on to fix a retiring age for professors, which had not previously been done. The age of compulsory retirement is fixed at sixty-five. But it is impossible to impose compulsory retirement on a man who has spent himself in good service at a very modest salary unless some provision is made for pensioning him. The University, therefore, arranged a superannuation scheme, on which the best advice in the city was called in. The superannuation fund is mainly formed by deductions from the professors' salaries, but these contributions are to some extent supplemented by contributions from the University, varying in amount, but in no case amounting to more than £16 per annum. Under this scheme a professor who is compulsorily retired at sixty-five, after spending the best of his life in the service of the University, may consider himself very fortunate if he gets an annuity of £200 per annum for the rest of his life. It will be agreed that this is not an extravagant provision. But nobody takes up University teaching in the hope of making money out of it, or for any other reason than that his heart is in his work. Every University teacher who is so far successful as to rise to a professorship knows that he could make a larger income and a better provision for his children in another kind of work. He sticks to his work because it is so much its own reward.

The salaries of junior teachers range from £100 to £350 per annum; only a very few reach the higher figure, and the usual salary of a young University teacher is £150. It will be admitted that this is not an excessive amount. Why is it that young men of exceptional ability will accept such salaries, when they could get much more elsewhere? The reason is three-fold: first, because they are earning the experience which will qualify them for better paid work; secondly, because they have, in a University, the opportunity of doing original work by which they can earn a reputation

D

supply of first-class men, is apt to be obscure. ... difficulty is that the Universities all have to ... do with their money that everything has to ... cheaply as possible.

It is a rather delicate matter to discuss in ... incomes of a number of our fellow-citizens, but the ... have a right to know these things. It is rather ... delicate to discuss the intellectual distinction of the ... of men whom the foundation of the University has placed in Liverpool. But it may at least be said that Liverpool has been singularly fortunate in the quality of the men whom she has succeeded in attracting, some of whom have been drawn here largely by the belief that no English city shows a more enlightened or a more promising attitude on higher education, while others have remained, in spite of the strongest financial temptations to go elsewhere, because of their enthusiasm for their work and their belief that very great things are to be expected of the University of Liverpool. Some of those who have left us are now so famous that their names have penetrated far beyond the world of learning, such as Sir Oliver Lodge, A. C. Bradley, Walter Raleigh, or A. R. Forsyth. But there are men as great in their own ways still among us, as the world outside has testified. Within the last two or three years three of our professors have been invited by Government to serve as the experts on important Royal Commissions. Others have received similar invitations from foreign Governments. Yet others are famous as authorities on their subjects throughout Europe and America, though often enough they are almost unknown to the general public in Liverpool. Not long ago the *Journal des Débats*, one of the principal newspapers in

France, devoted its front page to an article on the epoch-making discoveries of a Liverpool professor whose name never appears in the Liverpool newspapers. The important and authoritative books which our professors have published in the last few years would form a little library of the most remarkable range of interest. The list of the distinctions which learned bodies have bestowed upon them would form an astonishing catalogue.

... of the main thoroughfare, in the neighbourhood which lies between [...] Pembroke Place. No tramway actually [...] Brownlow Hill is a street that few [...] reasons, and none for pleasure; so that nobody [...] University except those who have something [...] to do there. This is in many ways a misfortune. University were a great pillared granite pile [...] of the city, challenging St. George's Hall, it [...] more constantly to the imagination of the citizens; [...] have built it in that way would have involved [...] the available money on stone and lime; it has been spent on men. If it had been planted among [...] lawns somewhere on the outskirts of the town, it would [...] been a pleasanter and more peaceful place; but the distance from railway stations and from the great [...] of tramway routes would have made it very inaccessible [...] students.

Not only is it rather hidden away, but no one would pretend that it is beautiful. It is built all of brick, [...] with smoke from the railway cutting that breaks into [...] corner of the quadrangle. Mean houses surround it, [...] the grim, vast workhouse faces it. There has been [...] extravagance here in external decoration; everything [...] clearly meant for work, and not for show.

Yet, though the inquisitive visitor will not find [...] charm of the gardens and cloisters of Oxford, he will [...] other very wonderful things. Few of the citizens of Liverpool, apart from those who are actually concerned in the work of the University (and not all even of these), have any notion of the lavish expenditure of time, thought, and money which has been made, or of the magnitude and richness of the provision here afforded for giving the highest kind of teaching to all who are capable of profiting by it. Unpretending though they are on an external view, the total cost of the buildings of the University and of their equipment has been over £334,000. The whole of this vast sum has been provided by the munificence of private donors. And when it is remembered that private donors have also provided the endowments on which the professors are maintained who direct the work that goes on in these buildings, the whole represents a colossal gift to the city. It represents, also, a great faith, and a great foresight of the needs of the new age.

At the risk of tediousness, it may be desirable to enumerate the principal buildings, and to describe the purposes to which they are developed. First comes the Victoria Building, erected at a cost of £54,000, with which (as many meetings are held there) Liverpool men are perhaps most familiar. It is named in honour of the late Queen, because it was planned in the year of her first jubilee, and includes as its principal architectural feature the clock tower by which in that year the citizens commemorated their loyalty. It includes also a fine library, built and in part endowed by the late Sir Henry Tate. It also contains class-rooms for the Faculty of Arts; but since the building was opened, in 1892, that faculty has grown so rapidly that it has overflowed into the original temporary building, filled that, and now occupies some houses in the neighbourhood as well. For the adequate accommodation of the Faculty of Arts a sum of £25,000 has been already provided, with which a new building is shortly to be erected, continuing the Victoria Building, but at right angles with it. Connected with the Victoria Building over an archway are the fine Engineering Laboratories, built by the late Sir Andrew Walker at a cost of £23,255; they also have become too small. On the other side of the quadrangle, facing the buildings already named, there is a remarkable continuous series of great laboratories. First come the George Holt

...ally, the research department of the laboratories... to these laboratories some the princely Institute of Physiology and Pathology, which have no equal in this country, and which were founded by the late Mr. Thompson Yates at a cost of £32,576. Beyond these, an archway, we come to the new building of the Dental School, recently erected at a cost of £26,379, in place of outworn old sheds in which medical students had previously worked. Next, in a little room, lies the newest of the series, built by Mr. E. K. Muspratt, at a cost of some £15,000. These are the only laboratories of their kind in England; Mr. Muspratt, himself a scientific chemist, knew that this branch of chemistry was to become of increasing importance to the industry of England, and he has ensured that his own city should be ahead of all England in meeting this new need. Finally, the quadrangle is closed by the long range of the Laboratories of General Chemistry, which have cost altogether £28,696. But the University has, some time since, spread beyond its original spacious quadrangle; and on the other side of Brownlow Street we find the perfectly equipped Laboratory of Botany, for which Mr. W. P. Hartley gave £13,500, and the huge Laboratories of Zoology and Electrotechnics, built at a cost of £30,175.

This impressive range of buildings represents a very great expenditure of money. But that expenditure has placed Liverpool in the forefront of English cities in the provision of the most complete facilities for advanced studies, and especially for those studies upon which national efficiency depends. If, however, the outer shell of these great buildings

has been costly, the equipment of them with the apparatus
and material necessary for work of the highest quality is
proportionately still more costly. In almost every case
the generous donors have supplied equipment as well as
buildings; but equipment needs renewing, and it needs
extension as knowledge grows. Hence the provision of the
apparatus and material for teaching is a constant drain upon
the resources of the University. Such expenditure is
jealously guarded, and there is scarcely a teacher in the
University who, if asked, would not say that his department
was ill-equipped in comparison with similar departments in
great German or American Universities, though he would
probably at the same time boast that it compared favourably
with most other Universities in the United Kingdom. The
truth is that the English people has hitherto scarcely begun
to realise how necessary this higher teaching is, and how
costly it must be if it is to be efficient. More advanced
teaching is necessarily more costly than less advanced, not
only because the student has to be taught more, and more
difficult, things, but still more because the only real method
of teaching him is to put instruments and materials at his
disposal, and guide him into the way of finding out truth
for himself. The object of a University training is not so
much to communicate established facts as to cultivate in the
student the habit and faculty of independent judgment and
investigation. And that is by far the more costly, as it is
by far the more valuable process. It involves great space
for the student to work in; it involves apparatus and
materials sufficient to enable him to perform all kinds of
operations; it involves, finally, the provision of skilled aid,
not only to instruct him in set lectures, but also to guide
him in applying for himself the principles which the lectures
have laid down.

But every new laboratory or other building with which
the generosity of wealthy donors supplies the University
involves it in additional expense not only for scientific
equipment, but also for rates, lighting, cleaning, and
so forth; humdrum expenditures which do not attract

benevolence, but which must somehow be met. They cannot be met out of students' fees, because every student costs more than he pays here, as in every other University in the world; the rapid increase of the student has, therefore, meant a steady increase of necessary expenditure.

Liverpool affords few experiences of greater interest than a tour through this great range of buildings, unpretending outside, but finely equipped, and full of busy students and investigators. The citizen should certainly seize any opportunity of visiting them that may offer; he will be welcomed if he comes at a convenient time. Unfortunately it is usually impossible to receive visitors when work is in full swing, because their appearance in any numbers would prove a serious interruption. But if the visitor could come then, he would note two things. He would find that while some of the newer buildings are not yet full, and afford room for considerable expansion, all the older buildings are overcrowded, so that it is sometimes difficult to find a place in which to hold a class or to accommodate students at their practical work. Nowhere is this more marked than in the Victoria Building, which was erected as recently as 1892, and was then supposed to provide ample room for further expansion. Its rooms are now too small for the classes which have to be held in them; its library has not seats enough to contain the students who read in it, though subsidiary class-libraries have been provided. In short, rapidly as the buildings of the University have grown, they have scarcely grown rapidly enough to meet the increase in the number of students and the growth of the multifarious activities of which a university in a great city tends increasingly to make itself the centre.

V. COURSES OF STUDY AND RESEARCH.

The most important test of the efficiency of a University is to be found in the answer to the questions, not " How many students has it ?" or " How many teachers has it ?" or " How big and how many are its buildings ?" but " How and what does it teach its students ?" and " What is it doing to advance human knowledge ?"

For the purposes of teaching and research, the University of Liverpool is divided into five " faculties," together with several " schools," more or less separately organised. Each of the faculties and two of the schools grant different degrees ; so that the " Bachelor's," or first degree, is granted under seven different titles, and there is a corresponding number of higher degrees, Master's and Doctor's. Here at once emerges a striking contrast between the methods of the University of Liverpool (and, indeed, of all the modern Universities) and those of the old Universities of Oxford and Cambridge. In the old Universities every undergraduate is reading for the same degree, that of B.A. ; and from this fact many have assumed that the old Universities provide a much more " liberal " or " cultural " education. But this impression is not really borne out when we come to examine the facts. It is true that a much larger proportion of Oxford and Cambridge men are reading what are called Arts subjects. But it is also true that the B.A. degree of Oxford and Cambridge may mean quite as specialised and even technical a course as the special degrees of Liverpool. In Oxford a man may spend his time mainly in the study of comparative morphology, and still receive the B.A. In Liverpool he would be called B.Sc. In Cambridge a man may follow a course of specialised study in engineering, and still receive the B.A. In Liverpool he would be called B.Eng., without having taken a course at all more technical in character. Opinions may differ as to the relative merits of these two systems of nomenclature. In Liverpool, as in all the modern Universities, the principle adopted is that a

... Bachelor of Medicine ... ...
But, after all, these are mere questions ... ...
things that we are concerned with, not ... ...
letters a student is allowed to write after his ...
has finished his course, but what he learns ...

The various kinds of degree and diploma ...
be grouped under two heads, which are quite ...
First come what may be called the two "primary" ...
of Arts and Science, upon which all the rest ...
in which pure knowledge is taught, irrespective of ...
applications. In the one, Man as a thinking being, ...
all his activities, is studied; and history, literature, ...
languages, philosophy, and economics belong to the Faculty
of Arts. In the other, Nature is studied; and mathematics,
physics, chemistry, and biology belong to the Faculty of
Science. While in the professional faculties a student is
bound to go through a practically fixed course in which there
is little variation, in the primary faculties there is inevitably
a very great variety in the character of the courses which
a student may take. One broad distinction especially stands
out, between the Ordinary degree, which represents a
moderate degree of proficiency in a considerable range of
subjects, and an Honours degree, which represents a much
higher proficiency in a special subject or group of subjects.

The great majority of the students take Ordinary degrees,
and it has throughout been the policy of the University to
make the Ordinary degree represent a really sound standard
of knowledge in the subjects which it covers. The "pass"
or "poll" degree of the older Universities admittedly
represent an exceedingly low standard; those of the modern
Universities have always been much higher, because the

modern Universities never have to deal with students who come to them merely for social reasons, and who have no intention of doing serious work. The standard at entrance of the modern Universities is much higher (except in Greek Grammar), and represents a much wider range, than that of the old Universities; and every student must have passed it before he begins to read for a degree, which is not the case at Oxford. The standard represented by the Ordinary degree is steadily rising, and will continue to rise in proportion to the improvement of the general level of education below the University grade. For it is a sound principle that only students who are really worth cultivating should be admitted to share in the privileges of a civic University.

The fact that the Ordinary degree represents a substantial degree of attainment has made it possible to exclude from the Honours schools all but picked students. In Oxford every student of any ability takes an Honours degree, and the third and fourth classes are very populous. In Liverpool, students are discouraged from reading for an Honours degree unless they seem likely to be able to obtain a first or second class; for, except in that case, it will be more to their advantage in every way to take an Ordinary degree. Consequently the Honours students are few, though their numbers are rapidly growing.

It would be out of place, in this article, to analyse the various courses which it is possible for a student to pursue. But one or two general observations may be made. In the first place, the University of Liverpool has struck out a new line in requiring from all Honours students not only the kind of book-knowledge which can be tested by examination papers, but also evidence of their capacity to do original and independent work in their subjects. This has long been required in the Faculty of Science, where laboratory equipment makes it easy to organise. But the same principle has been extended, in Liverpool alone among British Universities, to the Honours schools of the Faculty of Arts, in which a dissertation, prepared by the student during his course, has to be submitted to the examiners, and the student must undergo a searching oral examination, in addition to written examination, on his work. An attempt is now being made to introduce this system in Oxford, and the example of Liverpool has been much quoted.

All examinations, whether Ordinary or Honours, are conducted in co-operation by the teachers and by external examiners, among whom are many of the most distinguished scholars in their subjects in England—men with an intimate knowledge of the methods and standards of other Universities. It is clearly understood that part of the business of the external examiner is to ensure that the standard shall not be in any way lower than that of other Universities; and for that purpose these examiners have an absolute right of veto.

It is perhaps in regard to the courses of study leading up to definite professions that the most distinctive features of the system of the new Universities are to be found. Not content with providing teaching for the ancient professions of medicine and law, the new Universities feel it to be their duty to provide instruction for the new professions of the modern world as well. In this respect they are following the precedent set by the American Universities. In Germany the course of training for men who are to become engineers, or technical chemists, or commercial men are conducted in great technical Universities, not by the Universities proper. But this is not only a wasteful system (since it involves the duplication of a large part of the teaching staff), but it is also unfortunate in its effects on the students. For it is a good thing for students of many varied types to be blended; it is a bad thing for those who are going in for a particular profession to be herded apart during their period of training. When the great German chemist Ostwald was here, he said that what struck him most about the modern English Universities was that, while they were as yet far behind the German Universities in respect to the magnitude of their equipments, they were in one respect far

ahead, in that in England the Universities were coming to
be recognised as the training grounds equally for all
professions, and so the technical student found his work
liberalised by contact with men who were pursuing knowledge
for knowledge's sake, and was taught by men who were not
primarily thinking of the technical applications of their
subjects. In a generation, he said, provided that England
continued to maintain her Universities with proper liberality,
this would very likely give her a material advantage over
Germany.

The University of Liverpool has very steadily set itself
to meet the needs of one new profession after another, and
now architects, veterinary doctors, dentists, and several
others have been provided for. Not all of these have degree
courses provided for them. Some of them work only for
diplomas, and therefore do not count among the " matriculated
students." Others, even in professions in which degrees
are given, work for diplomas given by outside bodies, such
as the R.C.P. or the R.C.S. But whatever the qualification
at which they aim, they are taught in precisely the same
way by highly-equipped specialists, each of whom deals with
his subject in a purely scientific spirit, and so makes it a
medium of culture and of intellectual training as well as an
equipment for practical work. That is to say, they are
taught in a University spirit.

This is a true and noble conception of a University,
which requires that it should be not merely the home of pure
scholars, studying solely for knowledge or for self-culture,
or of well-to-do, elegant idlers, but that, side by side with
these, it should provide efficient and generous training in the
business of their life for all types of men who have to work
with their brains. These men can be so trained that not
only will they be enabled to do their work well, but their
work will itself be not merely a means of livelihood, but a
perpetual delight and a continual educative power, because
its meaning and aims and relations with other professions

Besides communicating established knowledge and providing training for the professions, it is one of the functions of a University worthy of the name to ... knowledge in many different fields. How does the University of Liverpool fulfil this function? In the first place ... distinguished among English Universities by the number ... endowments which it possesses for the express purpose ... encouraging research. The professor of bio-chemistry ... purely a research professor—that is to say, his primary ... is to conduct research himself, and to guide and aid qualified persons who are willing to devote their time to that work. Round him there is a group of men conducting most valuable investigations at their own cost, and as a result the "Journal of Bio-chemistry," a learned quarterly devoted to this subject, is issued from Liverpool, which has thus become in some sense the centre of these studies. The professor and lecturer in tropical medicine are the centres and directors of a school of research whose fame has spread throughout the world and needs no celebration in Liverpool, which knows the value of its work. The recently-founded professorship and laboratory of physical chemistry, though they provide a good deal of instruction for ordinary students, exist primarily for the purpose of adding to our knowledge of a subject which is going to be of fundamental importance for many industries. The three professors of archæology are all men whose work is known throughout Europe, and who add every year to our knowledge of the remote past by their excavations. Nothing has more impressed the learned world recently than the spectacle of a trading town providing such magnificent equipment for the extension of human knowledge. All these activities have been endowed by private benefactors,

but they have earned for the name of Liverpool a new honour.

But it is not only in departments that exist primarily for research, or through the hundred and thirty post-graduate research students who are engaged in this work, that the University contributes to the advance of human knowledge. Of all the changes which the foundation of an independent University has brought about, none is more striking than the increased emphasis which is laid upon the importance of this function. There is no single teacher, senior or junior, to whom it is not daily brought home that he does not deserve his position unless he is doing his best to enlarge the bounds of knowledge; that he cannot even be a good University teacher unless he is also perpetually a learner and an explorer. And when any new teacher is appointed, one of the principal questions always asked is the question: What original work has he done, and what is he likely to do? There is no single department of the University in which original investigation is not being actively carried on. And it must not be imagined that this is at the cost of teaching; on the contrary, it gives a new inspiration to teaching and changes its character. For increasingly the student is made to feel that the principal thing which he has to learn is not merely to charge his memory with masses of established fact (though, of course, he must do this), but still more to learn how to discover truth for himself, to learn how to weigh evidence and how to test the validity of other men's conclusions. If the University were merely an organisation for filling men's minds with orderly and useful knowledge, it would no doubt be serving a very useful purpose. But what is most instructive about it and about other similar places—what makes the foundation of these new Universities promise a real renascence in England—is that the real modern University is far more than this. It tries to give its students not mere dogmatically-asserted conclusions, but to inspire them with the spirit of inquiry; it aims at sending out into the world a continuous succession of men competent and zealous for their work, and, above all, knowing how to look for the causes of the difficulties by which they may find themselves faced. Research and teaching cannot be treated separately, because the spirit of research is the thing most worth teaching.

VI. FINANCE AND GOVERNMENT.

The admirably full and clear financial statement which is annually issued by the University makes its position easy to understand.

Let us take, to begin with, its capital value. This now amounts to £735,000. The whole of this great sum (with the exception of the site, valued at £30,000, which was provided by the Corporation in 1881, when University College was founded) has been subscribed during the last twenty-five years by the generosity of private benefactors. It represents capital gifts to the value of nearly £30,000 on the average in every year since the college was founded. This is a degree of munificence for a great public object to which it would be hard to find a parallel in England, though in America it has been far surpassed in many cases. Certainly the citizens of Liverpool owe a deep debt to the generous men and women who have contributed so lavishly to the establishment of a great public institution for the public service. Yet even this great sum would be inadequate by itself for the organisation of an efficient University. It is a commonplace in America, where more fully than anywhere else in the Anglo-Saxon world the value of University education has been appreciated, that 5,000,000 dollars, or £1,000,000 sterling, is the smallest capital upon which an efficient university can be established. Though there are many inferior institutions of university rank in America, that country contains at least twenty which are equipped with an amplitude unknown in this country; and every great American city, like New York, Boston, Philadelphia, Chicago, San Francisco, Baltimore, prides itself upon possessing a university (and in some cases two or even three universities), each of which is endowed with four or five times the "minimum" of a million sterling. If, therefore, Liverpool's University is to be capable of comparison with the universities of its sister cities, the £735,000 of capital needs a good deal of supplementation. That this is so is clear when we come to analyse the way in which the capital has been expended. Over £330,000 has gone in sites and buildings; about £340,000 represents permanent endowments of professorships, lectureships, and scholarships; and the remainder includes the value of a hall of residence for students (£10,000), the fund of £8,000 which has been subscribed for the erection of a Students' Union, a sum of £25,000 set apart for a new building to be soon erected, the superannuation fund (£3,600), which has mainly been raised by deductions from the professors' salaries, and a number of minor items. Of the total capital, therefore, only about £340,000 yields an annual income, and this income is earmarked by the donors for specific purposes. Revenue for the ordinary running expenses of the University, and for the maintenance of every kind of work for which full endowments have not been provided, must be found elsewhere.

The annual income of the University is now £61,000. This income is drawn from four main sources. Over £17,000 per annum comes from the income of endowments; over £15,000 per annum from students' fees; nearly £2,000 from annual subscriptions for various purposes; and £26,000 from public funds. Roughly, half of the public money comes from Government, the other half from the Corporations of Liverpool, Birkenhead, and Bootle, and the County Councils of Lancashire and Cheshire, Liverpool being vastly the largest contributor. It may be noted that the Government grants are, with one exception (that of Manchester), the largest made to any grant-receiving university in England. This is the more satisfactory when it is remembered on what principles these grants are determined. They are made on the report of experts in consideration of two facts, firstly the efficiency of the University and the value of the work which it does, and, secondly, the extent of the local support which it receives. It is safe to prophesy that the amount of Government grants for University education will largely increase in the future, but it is also certain that the amount of them which will come to any particular place will continue to be determined partly in proportion to the generosity of the support locally given, and partly in proportion to the efficiency of the work done.

Three features in the analysis of the income of the University deserve special note. The first is that, in comparison ·with Oxford and Cambridge, a small part of the total income (not much more than one-fourth) is derived from income on endowments. This, of course, was inevitable, since a new University could not possibly hope, in a single generation, to obtain capital gifts that would compare with the accumulation of centuries; it was the more inevitable because at the outset so large a proportion of the capital expenditure must be on buildings, which are not merely not productive, but cause a heavy drain on general resources for upkeep and maintenance.

The second feature is that so large a proportion of the total is derived from fees. The student here pays on the average about one-fourth the cost of his education; in Oxford he pays perhaps one-sixth. This does not mean that the student here pays unduly high fees; on the contrary, the average fee paid is about the same as in other places of the same kind in England. Undeniably, it would be highly advantageous to bring about a reduction in the scale of fees; some would go so far as to advocate their total abolition. But it will be seen that it would be impossible to work the University efficiently without fees, the contribution from this source to the total expenditure being half as much again as the amount of the city grant. Fees, therefore, can only be very gradually reduced; and, since many students are quite well able to pay, there is much to be said for the view that the object of such a reduction— that of making a University education easily attainable to all promising students—could be better secured by an increase in the number of scholarships reserved for candidates who without them would be unable to proceed.

The third feature is the large proportion of the total income—not far short of one half—which is derived from public sources. This was absolutely necessary if new

universities were to be founded on an adequate scale. In
the opinion of all educationalists these public subsidies will
not only have to continue, but must even increase if England
is to equip herself on a scale at all comparable to that on
which her commercial rivals have equipped themselves. But
one interesting result of these grants of public money should
be noted. Public support means public interest, and also.
public control. The State and the municipalities have a
right to a far greater share in the control of these new
universities than they have ever had in the old; and, as we
shall see, they have received it—nowhere more fully than
in Liverpool. So the modern University is a popular
University in a sense, and to an extent hitherto unknown.

So much for income. Next we must note, in broad
outline, how this income is expended. The largest item is
for the salaries of teachers and examiners, which swallows
up over £29,000 per annum. If this sum were equally
divided among all the teachers whose whole time is devoted
to their work, each would receive a salary of about £333
per annum, which is certainly not excessive. But when it
is remembered that over thirty external examiners have to
receive fees, and that there is a very large number of teachers
who give part of their time to teaching work, and receive
some payment, it will be seen that the salary scale does
not err on the side of excessive liberality.

The next largest item is that of administration and
general expenses, amounting to over £12,000. This may
at first sight seem large, but not when the details are
examined. For it includes the salaries of the Vice-Chancellor,
the Registrar, the Bursar, the Librarian, and the Deans of
the five Faculties (which total £3,375); office staff, rates,
taxes, insurance, cleaning, repairs and renewals, printing,
advertising, stationery, postage, the expenses of ceremonies,
and the innumerable other small expenditures involved in
the upkeep of a great institution, as well as superannuation
grants (only £600), and grants in aid to student bodies and
to University extension lectures. There is perhaps no point

at which the careful economy of the University administration is more clearly shown than in these respects.

Next comes the cost of maintenance of the buildings and the provision of service and equipment and materials for the great scientific laboratories, which swallow up over £11,000. And lastly comes over £6,000 for scholarships and fellowships, which is the smallest of the big items, but might with great advantage be increased. It ought to be said, however, that the University authorities are always anxiously ready, so far as possible, to provide additional money for scholarships or grants in aid out of general funds in deserving cases when the funds specifically set aside have been exhausted. Some minor expenditures have been omitted. But the big items already enumerated practically swallow up the whole income, and it is only the most anxious care that enables a small balance to be handed over at the end of the year. There is certainly no money to spare. Extremely important and valuable new developments are constantly being asked for, and constantly have to be refused. Thus the University has as yet no regular provision for advanced teaching in geology, a subject not only of the highest scientific importance, but of immense practical value in a mining district; or in Spanish,* though Liverpool is the chief centre of trade with the Spanish-speaking countries; or in Hebrew and other Oriental languages, which are of the first importance for men intending to enter the Church. This is no place in which to catalogue the necessary future developments, or the list might be very much extended. But perhaps enough has been said to show that, while the resources and equipment of the University have been doubled during the last four years, it is still far from being in a condition in which it will be possible to cry "Halt!" or to say that the vast population which is dependent for intellectual leadership on the city of Liverpool has received a provision

---

* Since this sentence was written, a generous bequest by the late Mr. J. L. Bowes has rendered possible the creation of a Lectureship in Spanish.

equal to that which similar communities possess in other countries.

A very few words must suffice to describe the mode in which the University is governed. It differs very widely from that in vogue in the older Universities. There the ultimate and supreme power is vested in the body of graduates, so that Oxford and Cambridge are close corporations, over whose action no outside body (except Parliament) can exercise any control; and as the body of graduates are for the most part highly conservative in temper, no really great change can be brought about except with the greatest difficulty, and the intending engineer must still cram his modicum of Greek grammar before beginning his studies, and the woman who has earned her degree is still denied it.

In Liverpool, the supreme body is the Court, a very large body of some 400 members, including all large donors, together with representatives of every University in the United Kingdom, of all the principal educational institutions in the neighbourhood, of City and Borough and County Councils, of Trades Councils, of every professional organisation, of every religious denomination, and, in short, of every body which is in any way concerned in educational or public work, or is in any way likely to be interested in or affected by the work carried on by the University. The Court meets at least twice a year, and all important new legislation has to be approved by it, while it receives every year the most detailed reports of the year's work. Naturally so large a body cannot consider most matters in much detail. But at least every organisation concerned is here provided with a means of expressing its views, and thus it may be hoped that the University will be prevented from getting out of touch with the needs and feelings of the people whom it serves. When the University is doing well, it may be expected that the meetings of the Court will be more or less formal. But when any question arises upon which there is deep feeling or difference of opinion, it will be expressed here. More than once this has already happened. Thus, when a scheme for training military officers was brought forward, it was rejected by a full meeting of the Court after a long debate.

The ordinary administration is vested in a smaller body —the Council—four-fifths of whose members are business men, the other fifth consisting of representatives of the academic body. Five members are directly appointed by the City Council, which is thus able to exercise a close influence on whatever is done. The other members include fourteen members elected by the Court (among whom are four city councillors), and the officers of the University— Lord Derby (the Chancellor), Sir E. Lawrence and Mr. E. K. Muspratt (the Pro-Chancellors), Mr. Hugh R. Rathbone (the treasurer), and the Vice-Chancellor. There is not a member of this powerful body whose name is not known and respected in Liverpool; and, in addition to the actual members of the City Council, it includes some of the greatest merchant princes of the city. It meets at least once a month, and has control of all the business of the University, taking especial care of the administration of finance.

After the Council comes the Senate, which is the supreme academic body, consisting of the whole body of professors. Except on some purely academic points, it can take no action without the approval of Council, but naturally its opinion has the greatest weight with Council. Finally, each of the five Faculties into which the University is divided has its meeting of teachers, called "the Faculty," for discussing and arranging work, and making suggestions and drawing up plans for development or advance. It is from the Faculties that the initiation of schemes or changes generally comes; then such proposals have to run the gauntlet of the criticism of members of other Faculties in Senate, and finally (if they survive so far) they come before the Council, and if approved by the Council, to the Court.

This is the main framework of University government. It is an elaborate system, but not more elaborate than that

of other Universities. And, on the whole, it seems as good
a system as could be devised for retaining all the enthusiasm
and knowledge of experts, combined with the cool criticism
and the ultimate control of those who have to find the means
and to consider how the funds at their disposal can be most
wisely administered. Thus, in its system of government, as
in its finance, the University of Liverpool is as representative
and as fully under popular control as is consistent with the
highly expert and specialised character of the work which it
has to do. No Universities in the history of education have
ever gone further in the direction of popular control than
these new English Universities; and it is but just to say
that so far experience justifies us in claiming that this
system has been more generous and more enlightened than
the narrower and more exclusively academic system which
until this generation was thought to be the only possible
form of University organisation.

VII. MISCELLANEOUS PUBLIC SERVICES.

In previous articles we have passed in review the number and character of the student body and of the teaching body of the University; we have glanced at its buildings and equipments; we have analysed its finance and described its mode of government; and we have noted the outstanding features of its systems of teaching and research. This list of topics might seem to be exhaustive, and in most cases it would be so. But a modern city University finds itself called upon to do many things beyond the training of those students who come to it for full courses of study. A modern University, planted like a lighthouse of knowledge in the midst of a vast population, cannot adequately perform the service which it owes to the community unless it makes itself a stimulator of the disinterested love of knowledge in every class, unless it makes itself the nucleus of every kind of effort for the intellectual advancement of the community, unless it makes the highest knowledge available for every kind of public service, and unless it succeeds in gradually permeating the whole of the community with respect for knowledge, and with the scientific attitude towards the facts of life. That will take centuries to accomplish; but in the meanwhile, let us see how the University of Liverpool is addressing itself to these responsibilities.

First of all, it forms a natural meeting-place for those scattered enthusiasts whose zeal for knowledge might be wasted (except for their own pleasure) unless they were enabled to utilise it by co-operation. Such men have always existed in considerable numbers. They are, in some ways, the salt of such a city as ours, and long before the University was founded societies existed for their use, such as the Literary and Philosophical Society, or the Historic Society of Lancashire and Cheshire, which have done invaluable work. With these the University has always been careful to avoid any appearance of rivalry or competition. But in other fields work remained for it to do. Local amateurs of

professional work without adequate training or equipment have all by these means been enabled to draw upon the resources of the University. More recently a powerful organisation among working men, known as the Workers' Educational Association, has been formed for the express purpose of organising a demand for instruction for the working classes in those subjects by means of which life can be made richer, and the duties and privileges of citizenship brought home more fully. This body is working in the most intimate co-operation with the University, which is eager to do everything in its power to help.

Perhaps the field in which the general public service of the University is most clearly exhibited is in its relation to the other parts of the system of education. The existence of a University renders possible the upbuilding in this district of an educational system complete from top to bottom, and at every point this system can gain enormously from the existence and influence of the University. In the first place, every local education authority within a wide radius includes a representative of the University, and it is obvious that these representatives can often render most useful service to the bodies on which they serve by their knowledge of educational needs, and of the standard of attainment which ought to be aimed at. Again, the matriculation, or entrance, standard of the University represents the natural goal towards which the work of the other educational grades should be directed. The matriculation examination is increasingly coming to be accepted as the leaving examination of the schools, and as the examination in which higher public scholarships can most conveniently be awarded. It affords a single common standard, tending to equate the work of the secondary schools, while by its system of higher alternative papers it encourages the more ambitious schools to do higher work. This standard is as high as that exacted in any University, but it will advance as the secondary schools improve. In course of time it may be found possible to work out a good system of leaving certificates for schools which will render

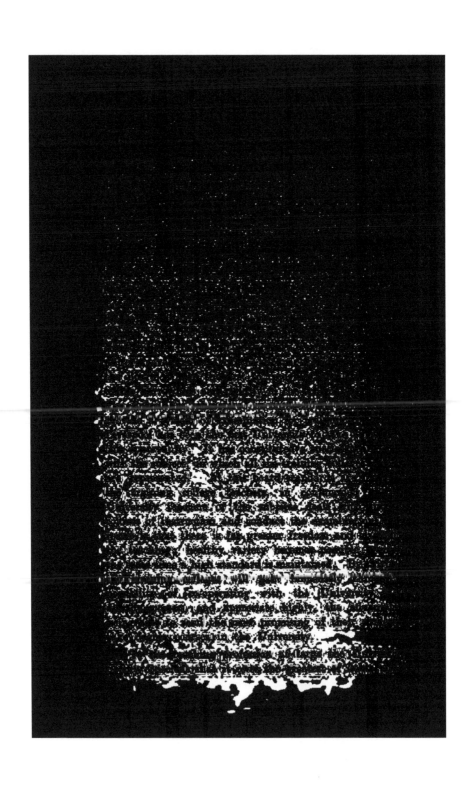

most imperative of duties. A city university is bound to try
to make itself a source of help and guidance in the problems
with which the teacher is faced; and this feeling has led to
the foundation of a remarkable organisation, which has no
parallel anywhere else in England. This is the Liverpool
Guild of Education, which has its headquarters at the
University, the Vice-Chancellor being its president. This
body aims at including in its membership all teachers of all
grades who seriously care about their professional work, as
well as members of education committees, inspectors, officials,
and others concerned in educational administration. It
will thus provide a meeting-place where all kinds of
educational questions can be freely discussed, where people
engaged in different branches of educational work can learn
to understand one another's methods and ideals, and where
great authorities or prophets can find a platform for the
exposition of their ideas. Affiliated to the general guild are
a number of special societies for discussing the methods of
treating the various special subjects in the school curriculum.
There are already six of these, and their number will soon
be increased. It is scarcely possible to exaggerate the
advantage which teachers and administrators may derive in
their work from the interchange of views and experience
which this organisation will render possible, and from the
knowledge and resources of the University which it will
place at their disposal. Already the Guild of Education
numbers many hundreds of members; they may in the
future be numbered by thousands.

But the teaching profession is not the only profession to
which the University renders services of this kind. Though
it is precluded by the terms of its charter from giving
instruction in theological subjects, it can and does render
services to the clergy. The Board of Biblical Studies, which,
though not formally a part of the University, is yet intimately
connected with it, and holds its classes in the University
buildings, is an organisation in which all denominations have
joined to provide instruction for working clergymen on the
sacred tongues, on the history of the Churches, and on the

contributions which modern scholarship has made to the interpretation of the Bible. It is a striking thing to find so many men of various schools of thought joining together in a spirit of friendship under the ægis of the University to study the great subjects on which they do not differ, and in which they are all equally concerned. A service of a kindred nature is that which the University is now undertaking at the request of a committee including both Churchmen and Dissenters—that of providing instruction for Sunday school teachers in the methods and art of teaching. These teachers will not receive any instruction in theology; they will simply be helped to teach more efficiently whatever they undertake to teach. Again, the only theological college in the neighbourhood—St. Aidan's, College, Birkenhead—is now affiliated to the University, and it is hoped that the result of this will be that after a while, instead of being content with a short two years of training in general as well as theological subjects, all the students of that college will take full degree courses in the University, their own college adding the theological training. The consequence of this will be a great improvement in the intellectual equipment of men taking up church work. What is being done in the case of St. Aidan's, could equally well be done in the case of other denominational colleges—the more of them the better.

To the medical profession the services of the University are still more direct. Its magnificently-equipped laboratories of medical science are open to them, and they may pursue their investigations into cases which perplex them. Short holiday courses are provided at intervals for general practitioners, to enable them to learn the most recent results of medical science and the latest methods of treatment. And a special organisation has been created whereby the practising doctor, doubtful about his diagnosis of a case, may send to the University a drop or two of his patient's blood, or other specimen, for careful analysis, and so be saved from serious blunders in treatment. In the Bacteriological Department "cultures" are made of the various disease germs, and in

those diseases which lend themselves to treatment in this way
serum can be there obtained to check the ravages of epidemics.
When, a few years ago, plague broke out at Cape Town,
Liverpool was the only place in the British Empire capable
of supplying the means of dealing with the outbreak.

Space does not permit of any account of the work done
in the Institute of Comparative Pathology, an offshoot of
the University devoted to scientific investigation of the
diseases of animals; but it must be obvious how important
this work is to the general health of the community, and
also to the interests of that great trade in animals of which
Liverpool is the centre. Again, it would be impossible to
exaggerate the advantage to the city of being able to utilise
the expert knowledge and the splendid laboratories of the
University for the conduct of the bacteriological analysis of
foods, milk, and water. But for the existence of the
University such analyses would be impossible without an
enormous expenditure on the part of the city for the provision
of staff and laboratories. These may serve as illustrations
(they are no more) of the way in which the existence of the
University places at the disposal of the government and
trade of the city the highest scientific skill and knowledge.
It would be easy to multiply examples of this; every day
applications are made to one or other department of the
University to test the strength of materials in the engineering
laboratories, to analyse the properties of possible new
commercial products, to explain the causes of unforeseen
defects in processes of manufacture. Not long ago, for
example, a mysterious ailment broke out among the workmen
in a factory. The University was appealed to; and the
botanical department was able to explain that the ailment
was due to the poisonous character of a new kind of wood
which had been used in the equipment of the factory. There
is no need to remind Liverpool readers of the immense
services which have been rendered by the School of Tropical
Medicine in attacking the diseases which have hitherto
rendered some of the most productive parts of the earth
almost uninhabitable to white men, and in thus not only

saving thousands of lives, but also opening out many new possibilities of trade. Still more direct services to trade are being rendered by the kindred but less widely known Institute of Commercial Research in the Tropics, which utilises the resources of the University for the purposes of collecting and tabulating all kinds of information regarding the products and conditions of these regions, of investigating scientific problems arising in connection with trade, and of supplying scientific information and advice. Already it is true—and every year will make it truer—that, thanks to the University, there is scarcely any trade centre where the resources of science are more fully and more easily placed at the disposal of the merchant and the trader than in Liverpool.

But the University does not only provide stimulus and help for the learned professions; it does not only bring science to bear upon the problems of commerce; it is anxious also to bring the scientific spirit into operation in the investigation and treatment of the social problems which face every great aggregation of human beings like ours. The foundation of a University settlement forms, perhaps, the best means of getting into intimate and human contact with the elements of the social problem; and, young as it is, this organisation has already proved of great service in aiding in the work of several enterprises, such as the David Lewis Hostel and Club, and the Florence Institute. Closely related to this work is the School of Social Science, in which the University provides for men and women anxious to take part in social or administrative work instruction in the economic conditions which govern our society, in the character of the works of charity which are carried on, and their results, in the mode of organisation and the functions of the various bodies charged with local administration, in ethics as applied to citizenship, in the practical working of the poor law, and so forth. When this branch of University work develops as it ought to do we may, perhaps, hope to see the day when every city clergyman and every member of a public body will obtain something approaching to a

scientific knowledge of the conditions with which they have
to deal. And the spirit of sound and intelligent citizenship
which will thus be created will be still further stimulated by
that enlarged and more generous view of the history of the
city and the steps by which its present conditions have been
created which the work of the University School of Local
History, in conjunction with the independent work of many
devoted antiquaries, will gradually produce.

All the articles of this series have been of the nature
of broad and general summaries, but perhaps none of them
has been more summary in its character than this. For
when one tries to realise all the diverse and unrealised ways
in which the University not only can serve but is serving
the city, the theme grows to be too large for any article.
But perhaps enough has been said to show that the city's
University is a great deal more than a place of training for
the picked youth of the city in the work of their life. It
is capable of rendering incalculable services to innumerable
aspects of city life. And if it continues to be inspired by
the same generous ideals which have hitherto governed it,
it will become the nucleus and the inspiration of every
intellectual force that makes for progress. It will be
something far wider than the body of teachers and of students
who spend their days within its walls, for it will have linked
up with itself as in a great army an infinite diversity of
keen and intelligent spirits working for and dreaming of the
advance of the community along innumerable different lines.
It will be so vital an element in the city's life that it will
be almost impossible to imagine what the city would be
like without it. And it is the dim vision of this new ideal
of a University which accounts for the surprising enthusiasm
and generosity with which the University movement has been
taken up. For the creation of a University in the midst
of a trading town has not meant merely the provision of a
school of a higher kind; it has meant an enlargement of
civic ideals. Not without reason has it been said that
the University movement of the new century represents a
renascence likely to be as far reaching in its results as that

other Renascence of the fifteenth and sixteenth centuries, with all the portentous revolution which it brought in thought and life.   If that prophecy is a just one, Liverpool may well feel that the twenty-fifth anniversary of her University is as well worth celebrating as even the seven hundredth anniversary of her own civic liberties.   For if that prophecy is a just one, there has been no more fruitful advance made in all the seven centuries than the foundation of the city's University.